DBT Skills for Teens Made Simple

© Copyright Limitless Teen 2022 - All rights reserved.

The content contained within this book may not be reproduced, duplicated or transmitted without direct written permission from the author or the publisher.

Under no circumstances will any blame or legal responsibility be held against the publisher, or author, for any damages, reparation, or monetary loss due to the information contained within this book. Either directly or indirectly. You are responsible for your own choices, actions, and results.

Legal Notice:

This book is copyright protected. This book is only for personal use. You cannot amend, distribute, sell, use, quote or paraphrase any part, or the content within this book, without the consent of the author or publisher.

Disclaimer Notice:

Please note the information contained within this document is for educational and entertainment purposes only. All effort has been executed to present accurate, up to date, and reliable, complete information. No warranties of any kind are declared or implied. Readers acknowledge that the author is not engaging in the rendering of legal, financial, medical or professional advice. The content within this book has been derived from various sources. Please consult a licensed professional before attempting any techniques outlined in this book.

By reading this document, the reader agrees that under no circumstances is the author responsible for any losses, direct or indirect, which are incurred as a result of the use of the information contained within this document, including, but not limited to, — errors, omissions, or inaccuracies.

TABLE OF CONTENTS

Introduction..................................05

Part 1: Mindfulness Skills for Building a Foundation (Days 1-7) 09

Day 1: Setting Your "Wise Mind" Goal 11

Day 2: Mindful Breathing 14

Day 3: observing Emotions....17

Day 4: Practicing Radical Acceptance 22

Day 5: Self- Compassion Check- In..............................28

Day 6: Mastering The STCPP Technique 33

Day 7: Mastering Mindful Listening 37

Part 2: Managing Anxiety with Emotion Regulation Skills 43

Day 8: 5-4-3-2-1 Grounding Technique 44

Day 9: Thought- Checking & Reframing.............................47

Day 10: Box Breathing 53

Day 11: Visualization For Calm 56

Day 12: Positive Affirmations.....61

Day 13: Progressive Muscle Relaxation 66

Day 14: Letting Go Of Worry Thoughts 70

Day 15: Self- Reflection On Anxiety Management 75

Part 3: Controlling Impulses with Distress Tolerance Skills (Days 16-23) 76

Day 16: Urge Surfing 78

Day 17: Pause and Choose 84

Day 18: Breaking Down Tasks 89

Day 19: Managing Distractions 95

Day 20: Mindful Eating 99

Day 21: Technology Boundaries.....................................103

Day 22: Counting Technique.................................107

Day 23: Reflecting on Impulse Control 110

Part 4: Boosting Emotional Health with Interpersonal Effectiveness Skills (Days 24-30) 111

Day 24: Practicing Gratitude 112

Day 25: Visualization for Success 115

Day 26: Acts of Kindness 118

Day 27: Journaling for Emotional Release 121

Day 28: Catching Wins 124

Day 29: Future Self Visualization 127

Day 30: Celebrating and Reflecting on Progress 130

4

Introduction

Hey there! Welcome to DBT Skills for Teens Made Simple. This isn't just any book—it's a hands-on guide to help you feel more in control, stay calm, and boost your confidence no matter what life throws your way.

If you're here, chances are you've felt anxious, overwhelmed, or maybe even struggled to handle intense emotions or impulses. You're definitely not alone, and you're in the right place.

DBT (Dialectical Behavior Therapy) might sound like a mouthful, but it's a super practical way to manage those tough moments and build skills you can use every single day.

Think of this as your own personal toolbox, packed with skills that help you handle anxiety, strengthen your relationships, make smart choices, and feel better in your own skin. You don't have to tackle everything at once, either. This book is designed as a 30-day journey, giving you just one skill to practice each day. It's like building a solid foundation, one brick at a time.

Each day, you'll dive into a new exercise that takes just 10 minutes. From quick ways to stay calm, like mindful breathing and grounding, to mastering impulse control with skills like urge surfing and mindful pauses, you'll find tools here that work in real-life situations—whether it's managing the stress of school, dealing with tough social situations, or just feeling good about yourself.

This book is for you if:

You're ready to tackle anxiety and feel more in control of your mind.

You'd like to build confidence and find balance with your emotions.

You want to learn how to pause, think, and respond (instead of reacting impulsively).

These DBT skills aren't just theories; they're meant to be used. By the end of 30 days, you'll have a toolkit of skills to carry with you for life, helping you face challenges with confidence, manage emotions, and stay grounded.

So grab a pen, make some space, and get ready to dig in. Remember, each day's skill is a small step toward feeling more in control, more confident, and more like you. Here's to a journey of self-discovery, growth, and strength. Let's get started!

Part 1: Mindfulness Skills for Building a Foundation (Days 1-7)

Welcome to the start of your journey! We're kicking off with mindfulness skills because they're the foundation for everything else you'll learn. Mindfulness isn't just about sitting still or meditating; it's about training your mind to stay present and focused, especially when things get overwhelming.

If you're dealing with anxiety, intense emotions, or impulses that feel hard to control, mindfulness can be like a superpower—it helps you tune into what's happening inside you without getting lost in it.

Over the next seven days, you'll learn to take a pause, breathe, and truly notice your thoughts and feelings without judgment. These skills will help you stay grounded in the moment, make decisions more thoughtfully, and feel more in control, even during life's ups and downs. Think of this as building a solid foundation that you can lean on whenever things get tough. Ready to dive in? Let's go!

Day 1: Setting Your "Wise Mind" Goal

Today, we're starting with one of the core ideas in DBT—finding your "Wise Mind." If you're feeling anxious, impulsive, or just overwhelmed by emotions, it can be hard to make clear decisions and stay grounded. A Wise Mind goal is a personal goal that combines both how you feel (your emotions) and what makes sense (your logic). In DBT, "Wise Mind" is that calm, clear-thinking part of you where your emotions and logical thinking work together to help you make good choices.

Setting your Wise Mind goal will help guide you over the next 30 days, reminding you of what you're working toward and why it matters.

Write down the goal that feels most meaningful to you.	**Examples** **Handling Anxiety** "I want to feel calmer and in control when I start to feel anxious." **Impulse Control** "I want to pause and think before reacting, especially when I'm frustrated."
Write a sentence or two describing what this goal looks like when you achieve it	**handling anxiety** staying calm before a test or meeting new people without feeling overwhelmed. **impulse control** Taking a deep breath before reacting in a disagreement with a friend or family member.

Check In with Your Goal Each Morning

Every morning, take a quick moment to remind yourself of your Wise Mind goal. Think about how practicing today's skill will help bring you closer to it. This simple check-in helps you stay motivated, making it easier to put in the effort each day. Over the next 30 days, watch how your goal starts to feel more and more achievable.

Day 2: Mindful Breathing

Today's skill is all about something super simple yet incredibly powerful. If you've ever felt your heart race before a test, gotten overwhelmed with emotions, or wanted to calm down but didn't know how—this skill is for you.

Mindful breathing gives you a way to hit the "pause" button on stress. It's like having a built-in tool to help you stay calm and in control, no matter what's happening around you. Taking just a few slow, deep breaths can help you get out of your head, release tension, and bring you back to the present moment. Whether you're facing an exam, dealing with friend drama, or just need a break from anxious thoughts, mindful breathing is a skill you can use anytime, anywhere.

Take 5 Mindful Breaths

1. Sit comfortably and let your hands rest on your legs or stomach.

2. Breathe in through your nose, counting to 4 in your head. Let the air fill your lungs and feel your belly expand

4. Breathe out through your mouth for 4 counts, feeling the air leaving your body and your muscles relaxing.

3. Pause for two seconds at the top of your breath.

5. Repeat: Take 5 slow, deep breaths this way, focusing only on the sensation of each inhale and exhale.

How to Use Mindful Breathing

During Social Situations
If you're feeling nervous or self-conscious in a group, try mindful breathing to steady your nerves. This helps you stay focused on the moment instead of worrying about what others think.

When You're Stressed or Angry
If you're upset or frustrated with someone, take a few deep breaths before you react. This gives you a second to pause, think clearly, and respond calmly instead of impulsively.

At Night Before Bed
When your mind is racing at night, use mindful breathing to quiet your thoughts and prepare for sleep. Focus on each breath and let go of any worries as you exhale.

Day 3: Observing Emotions

Observing emotions means noticing what you're feeling without letting those feelings control your reactions. When emotions like anxiety, anger, or sadness get intense, this skill helps you step back, understand why you're feeling this way, and choose a response that works for you.

It's especially helpful for managing school stress, friendship drama, and everyday ups and downs. Think of it as putting on a detective hat to study your emotions instead of letting them take over. By observing, you learn to understand your feelings without judging yourself.

Notice and Label Your Emotions

Step 1: Take a Pause

Draw a calming scene or write down three things that help you feel relaxed. Keep this page handy to remind you how to find calm quickly.

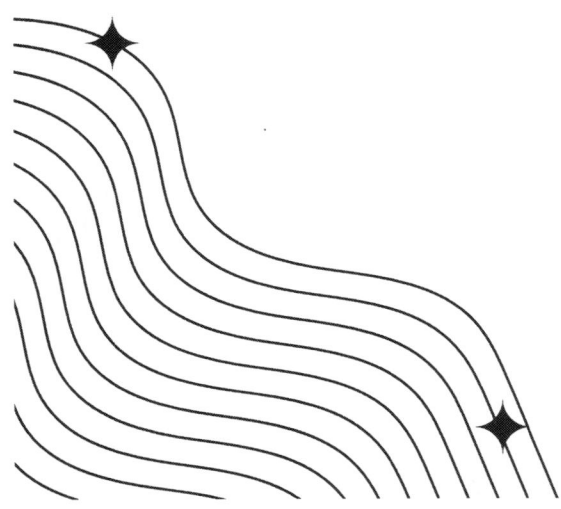

Step 2: Check In with Yourself

Ask yourself, "What am I feeling right now?" Don't worry if it feels a little messy—just notice. Write down whatever comes to mind in the space below.

_____
_____
_____
_____
_____
_____

Step 3: Label Your Emotions

Circle or color in the words that match your feelings today:

Happy   Proud   Joyful   Inspired

Grateful   Anxious   Stressed   Sad

Overwhelmed   Nervous   Lonely   Tired

Confused   Insecure   Angry   Annoyed

Frustrated   Embarrassed   Hurt   Calm

Motivated   Irritated   Worried   Focused

Step 4: Notice Where You Feel It in Your Body

Draw where you feel it in your body.
I feel it in my... (e.g., "shoulders are tense," "heart is racing," "stomach is tight")

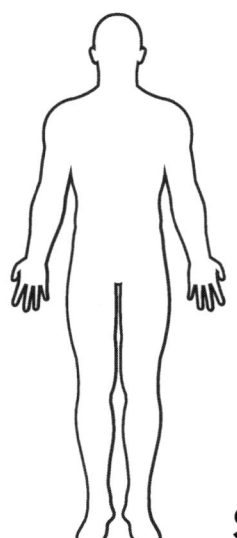

Step 5: Accept and Observe

Notice these feelings without judging yourself. Instead of thinking, "I shouldn't feel this way," try saying, "I'm noticing that I feel this way."

Write it down: Practice the phrase below to help you accept your emotions:

"I'm noticing that I feel_____. And that's okay."

How to Use Observing Emotions

When Arguing with Friends or Family
When anger rises in an argument with friends or family, label it: "I'm feeling angry and frustrated." Naming the emotion can help you stay calm and avoid reacting impulsively.

Dealing with Rejection or Disappointment
If you're feeling let down—like not making the team or getting a lower grade—acknowledge it by saying, "I'm feeling disappointed." This helps you accept your feelings instead of pushing them away.

At the End of the Day
Take a minute each evening to label any strong emotions you felt. This can reveal patterns and help you understand what triggers certain feelings.

Day 4: Practicing Radical Acceptance

Sometimes, things happen that we can't change, no matter how much we wish they were different. Maybe it's a family rule you don't agree with, a decision that didn't go your way, or even a feeling that won't go away. Radical acceptance is a skill that helps you make peace with reality as it is—rather than fighting against it. It doesn't mean you have to like or agree with the situation, but by accepting it, you can let go of some of the stress, anger, or frustration that comes with resistance.

Think of it like swimming with the current instead of against it. Practicing radical acceptance helps you save your energy for things you can change, making life feel less overwhelming and more manageable.

Letting Go of What You Can't Control

Step 1: Identify Something You're Struggling to Accept

Think about one situation or feeling that's hard for you to accept. Maybe it's a family rule, a disappointment, or something about yourself you wish were different. Notice how you feel about this situation. Remember, all feelings are okay—anger, frustration, sadness, or disappointment.

Write down what you're struggling to accept below. Be specific.

_____
_____
_____
_____
_____
_____
_____
_____

Step 2: Repeat an Acceptance Phrase

To help you with radical acceptance, choose a phrase that resonates with you and repeat it a few times.

Here are a few ideas:

"It is what it is."
"I can't change this, but I can change how I respond."
"I don't like this, but I can accept it."

write your chosen acceptance phrase here. Say it aloud, if you can.

_____
_____
_____
_____
_____

Step 3: Focus on Letting Go

Take a deep breath, and as you exhale, imagine releasing a bit of your resistance. Visualize letting go of the fight, even if it's just a little.

Step 4: Consider What You Can Control

Now that you've practiced acceptance, shift your focus to something you can control. For instance, while you might not change a family rule, you can choose how you react to it.

Write one thing you can control in this situation.
Example: "I can control my attitude by focusing on other fun things I can do."

_____
_____
_____

How to Use Radical Acceptance

During Family Disagreements
Let's say you and your family have different views on curfew or screen time rules. Instead of dwelling on how unfair it feels, try saying, "I don't agree with this, but I can accept that this is the rule right now." This helps you let go of constant frustration and focus on things you can control, like communicating your needs respectfully.

In Situations Beyond Your Control
Maybe a big event you were looking forward to got canceled, or a family trip didn't go as planned. Radical acceptance can help you avoid getting stuck in frustration. Try thinking, "I wish this were different, but I can't change it. I'll focus on what I can enjoy right now."

When Handling Emotions You Wish Would Go Away

Sometimes, you might feel sad, anxious, or frustrated for what feels like no reason. Instead of resisting or judging these feelings, try practicing radical acceptance: "I don't like feeling this way, but it's here, and that's okay." This helps you work through your feelings rather than fighting against them.

When Facing a Challenging Task

If you're dealing with a class or project that feels overwhelming, practice accepting that it's difficult but necessary. Instead of saying, "I hate this, and I can't do it," try, "This is hard, but I accept that I need to do it. I'll take it one step at a time."

💡 **Pro Tip:** Practicing radical acceptance doesn't mean giving up or ignoring your feelings. It's about acknowledging reality without letting frustration or disappointment control you.

Day 5: Self-Compassion Check-In

Self-compassion means being as kind to yourself as you would to your best friend. We all have moments when we feel anxious, mess up, or let our emotions get the best of us. It's easy to get caught up in thoughts like, "I messed up" or "I should've done better."

Self-compassion helps you replace that negative talk with kindness and encouragement. It's about being on your own team, no matter what.

Create Your "Power Statements" Board

Step 1: Think of What You Need to Hear

Think about a time when you've felt down on yourself. What would you want someone to say to you in that moment? Write down anything that comes to mind.

Examples:
"It's okay to make mistakes. I'm learning every day."
"I deserve kindness, especially when things are tough."

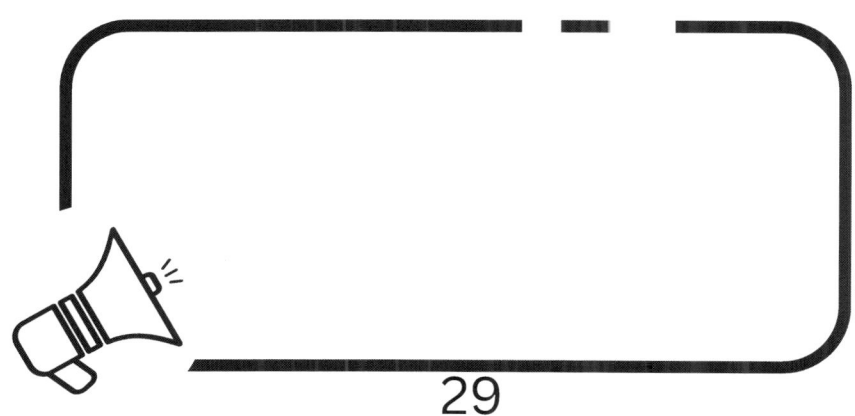

Step 2: Create Your Three Power Statements

Using what you wrote above, craft three personal affirmations that feel true and meaningful to you. These are your Power Statements!

Here are some ideas to inspire you:

"I am capable and strong, even when things are hard."
"I am allowed to take breaks and take care of myself."
"I have unique qualities that make me valuable."

Use the space below to write down three affirmations on "mini sticky notes" Decorate each one with small drawings, designs, or stickers to make them unique to you.

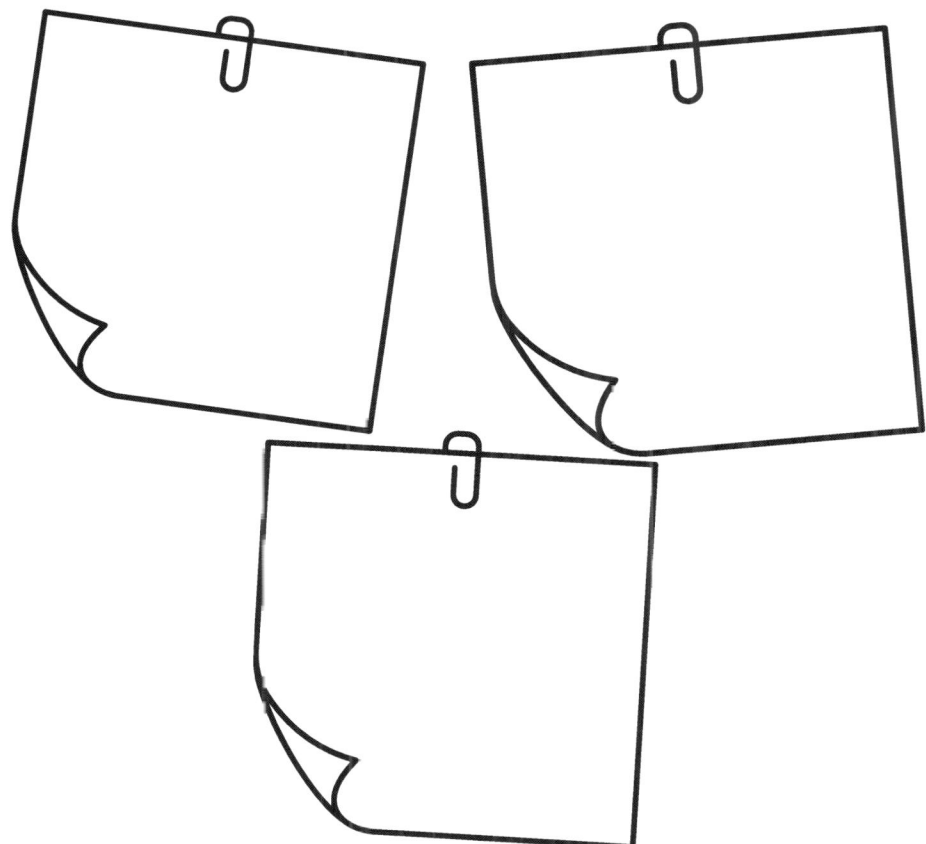

Frequently look back at your affirmations. Each time take a deep breath and repeat one of your affirmations. Notice how it feels to remind yourself of these positive words.

How to Use Your Power Statements

After a Mistake
If you're down after messing up, grab one of your affirmations to remind yourself that everyone makes mistakes. For example, read, "It's okay to make mistakes; I'm learning every day."

Anytime You Need Encouragement
Keep your affirmation jar or phone background handy so you can access a little positivity on tough days. Repeat your affirmation out loud or read it silently, noticing how it makes you feel

Before a Big Challenge
Use an affirmation as a quick boost of confidence. Try saying, "I am capable and strong, even when things are hard," before a test or presentation.

Day 6: Mastering the STOPP Technique

Ever find yourself reacting in the heat of the moment, only to regret it later? Maybe you said something in anger, acted impulsively, or let frustration get the best of you. The STOPP technique is a tool to help you pause, breathe, and think before you respond. It's like hitting a "reset button" in your brain, giving you time to choose a response instead of just reacting. This skill can make a huge difference when dealing with anxiety, big emotions, or situations that can lead to impulsive decisions.

S: Stop

Imagine a big red STOP sign in your mind. When you feel yourself getting upset, just pause—don't say or do anything right away. This helps prevent you from reacting on impulse.

T: Take a Breath

Take one or two deep, slow breaths. Breathing helps slow down your body's stress response and gives you a moment to calm down. Picture yourself letting go of some tension with each exhale.

 **O: Observe**

Notice what's happening around you and inside you. Ask yourself:

"What am I feeling right now?" (e.g., anger, frustration, hurt)

"What am I thinking right now?" (e.g., "They don't understand me," "This is so unfair")

"What's going on in my body?" (e.g., tight shoulders, clenched fists)

P: Pull Back

Take a step back mentally. Remind yourself of the bigger picture:
"Is this reaction helpful?"
"What would I say to a friend in this situation?"
"Will this matter as much tomorrow or next week?"
This part is all about gaining perspective, so you're not reacting solely from a place of emotion.

P: Practice What Works

Now that you've paused, calmed down, and observed your feelings, you can choose how to respond. Think about what will be most helpful:

Walk away from the situation if you need time to cool off.
Use a calm tone to communicate your feelings.
Decide if it's best to let it go and focus on something positive.

How to Use STOPP in Everyday Situations

If You're Tempted to React to Social Media

Maybe you saw a post that upset you or made you feel left out. Before you react impulsively (like posting something negative or sending an angry message), use STOPP to pause. Take a breath, observe your feelings, and pull back by reminding yourself that social media doesn't always show the full story. Choose what's best for your mental health.

When You're Anxious About School

If you're stressed about a test or assignment and feel your anxiety spiking, try using STOPP to calm yourself. Stop, take a few deep breaths, and observe your thoughts. Pull back and remind yourself that one test doesn't define you. Practice what works by breaking the work into smaller, manageable steps.

Day 7: Mastering Mindful Listening

Mindful listening is more than just hearing words—it's about being fully present and giving someone your undivided attention. When anxiety, stress, or impulses get in the way, it can be easy to interrupt, tune out, or jump in with advice. But when we listen mindfully, we improve our relationships and help others feel valued and understood.

Mindful Listening Practice

Step 1: Find a Listening Partner
Choose someone you feel comfortable with to practice listening.

Write their name here:

_____

Step 2: Be Fully Present
Put your phone away to make sure there are no distractions. Take a deep breath to focus.

Imagine a "pause button" to remind yourself to stay focused on them.

Step 3: Listen to Understand, Not to Respond

As they talk, focus entirely on them. Don't plan your response—just listen. Pay attention to:
- Their words
- Their tone of voice
- Their body language

Checklist: Did you...

☐ Make eye contact?

☐ Notice their tone of voice?

☐ Pay attention to their body language?

Step 4: Pause Before Responding

When they finish speaking, take a breath before you say anything. This pause helps you respond thoughtfully. If you're not sure how to respond, you can say, "I'm thinking about what you said."

Step 5: Show You're Listening

Nod, make eye contact, and say things like "I see" or "That makes sense." When it's your turn to speak, summarize what you heard. You could say something like, "It sounds like you're really frustrated with that situation."

Practice: "It sounds like you feel_____

because_____."

How to Use Mindful Listening

In Conversations with Friends
When your friend is venting about a tough day, use mindful listening to show you care. Put your phone away, make eye contact, and resist the urge to jump in with advice. Often, people just want to feel heard, not "fixed."

During Family Discussions
If you're in a conversation with family and feel yourself wanting to interrupt or defend your point, practice mindful listening instead. Focus on hearing them out first. This shows respect and makes family discussions more open and calm.

In Class or Group Projects
When working with classmates, listen mindfully to everyone's ideas without immediately

Weekly Reflection

Have you noticed any changes in handling stress or emotions?	What challenges did you face, and how did you overcome them?
Think about a moment where you used one of these skills. How did it change your response?	Learning new skills can be tough. What kept you going when things felt challenging?

Which skill was the most helpful? Why?

SET YOUR INTENTION FOR NEXT WEEK

Examples: "I'll use STOPP when I feel upset" or "I want to keep practicing mindful listening."

Part 2: Managing Anxiety with Emotion Regulation Skills

Welcome to Part 2 of your journey! This week, we'll focus on skills to help you manage anxiety and regulate intense emotions. If you've ever felt like your emotions are controlling you—whether it's worry, stress, or frustration—these skills will give you tools to feel more balanced and in control. These DBT techniques will teach you to handle emotions in a healthy way—facing anxiety without letting it control you, calming yourself in overwhelming moments, and making choices that keep you grounded.

Each day, you'll practice a new technique to help you feel more balanced and in control. By the end of this week, you'll have tools to manage anxiety and face challenges with greater calm and confidence. Let's get started!

Day 8: 5-4-3-2-1 Grounding Technique

Grounding is a technique that helps you stay in the present moment, especially when you're feeling anxious, overwhelmed, or stressed. When anxiety hits, your mind can race, making you feel disconnected from what's happening around you. Grounding brings you back to the "here and now" by engaging your senses. It's like pressing a reset button on your mind, helping you feel calmer and more centered.

The 5-4-3-2-1 technique is a fun, easy way to bring yourself back to the moment by noticing details around you that you might normally overlook. This technique can be done anywhere —before a test, a game, a social event, or whenever you need to calm down and refocus.

5 things you can see

4 things you can touch

3 things you can hear

2 things you can smell

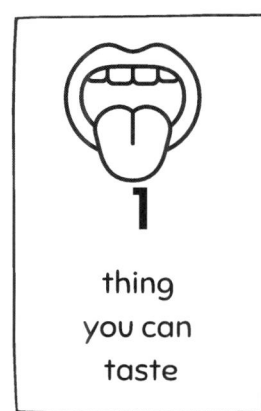
1 thing you can taste

Real-Life Application: How to Use the 5-4-3-2-1 Technique

Before a Test or Presentation
When nerves hit, do a quick round of 5-4-3-2-1 to bring yourself back to the room and away from worrying thoughts. It helps calm you so you can focus on what you know.

When You're Overwhelmed by Social Situations
If you're feeling nervous or self-conscious, use this technique to refocus. It helps you stay present instead of overthinking, giving you the confidence to just be yourself.

When Anxiety Hits at Night
If anxious thoughts keep you up, use this technique in bed to shift focus to what's around you instead of your worries. Noticing small details in your room can calm your mind for a better night's sleep.

Day 9: Thought-Checking and Reframing

We all have negative thoughts from time to time, especially during stressful or emotional moments. But sometimes these thoughts can become so automatic that they shape how we see ourselves and our abilities. Thought-checking and reframing helps you identify these negative patterns, challenge them, and replace them with more balanced, realistic perspectives.

This skill is especially helpful when you're feeling anxious, self-critical, or impulsive. By learning to reframe your thoughts, you're training yourself to think more positively and calmly, even in challenging situations.

Check the Facts: Reframe Your Thoughts

Spot the Negative Thought

Think of a recent situation that brought up a strong emotion or negative thought.
Example: "I feel like I'm going to fail this test."

_____
_____
_____

Describe Your Emotion

Write down what you're feeling. Be specific—are you anxious, frustrated, disappointed?
Example: "I feel really anxious and worried about failing."

_____
_____
_____

Ask Yourself Questions to Check the Facts

Answer these questions to see if your thought is based on facts or assumptions.

Is this thought based on facts or assumptions?

Example Answer: "It's mostly based on assumptions because I'm just guessing that I'll fail."

your answer:

_____
_____
_____

Is there any evidence supporting this thought?

Example Answer: "I've studied, and I understand a lot of the material, so I do have some knowledge."

Your Answer:

_____
_____
_____

Am I thinking in extremes (like "always" or "never" statements)?

Example Answer: "Yes, I'm saying 'I'll definitely fail,' which is an extreme thought."

Your Answer:

_____
_____
_____

What would I say to a friend in this situation?

Example Answer: "I'd tell a friend, 'You've prepared, so do your best and remember that one test doesn't define you.'"

Your Answer:

_____
_____
_____

Reframe the Thought Based on Facts

Using your answers, rewrite the thought in a balanced way. Try to make it realistic and supportive.
Example Balanced Thought:
"I studied and know most of the material. I might not get a perfect score, but I'm prepared, and I'll do my best."

Your Balanced Thought:

_____
_____
_____
_____
_____

Using Thought-Checking and Reframing Daily

When Comparing Yourself to Others
If you find yourself thinking, "They're so much better than me," reframe it as, "Everyone has different strengths, and I have mine too." This can help reduce self-doubt and boost confidence.

When Feeling Left Out or Rejected
If you're feeling down because you weren't included in plans, reframe a thought like "They don't like me" to something more balanced, like "This doesn't define my friendships. I have people who care about me."

Facing Self-Doubt
If a negative thought about your abilities keeps popping up, like "I'm not good enough," reframe it to, "I'm doing my best, and I'm learning and growing every day."

Day 10: Box Breathing

Box breathing is a powerful tool for managing anxiety and stress. It's called "box" breathing because each step is like a side of a box, creating a steady rhythm that can instantly help you feel more grounded. When anxiety or stress starts to build up, your body's natural response is to speed up your breathing and heart rate. Box breathing helps slow everything down, signaling to your brain that it's okay to relax.

This skill is super helpful when you're dealing with high-pressure moments, whether it's the big game, a tough exam, or any situation that makes you feel nervous. It's simple, effective, and can be done anywhere!

BOX BREATHING

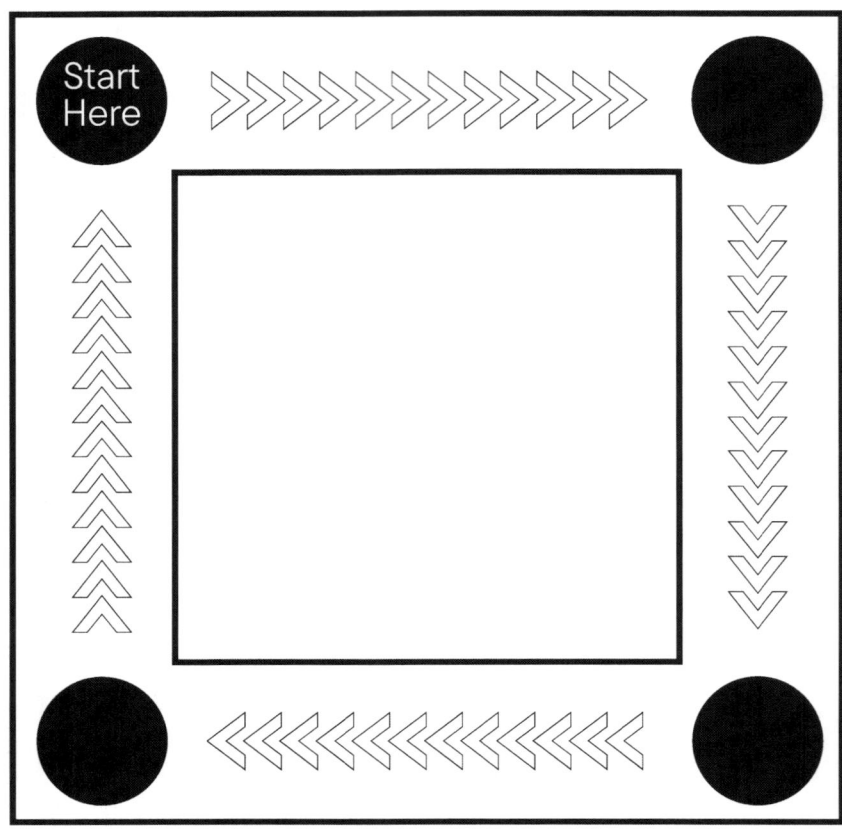

Place your finger on the dot that says "Start Here!" Take a deep breath in and count to 4. Pause and hold your breath for a count of 4. Move your finger to the next dot as you release your breath slowly through your mouth for 4 counts
Breathe in at each corner and count to 4 until you complete the box.

USING BOX BREATHING IN EVERYDAY SITUATIONS

When Feeling Overwhelmed by Homework or Tasks

If you're stressed about a big project or homework load, take a break to do some box breathing. This short reset can clear your mind, making it easier to tackle things one step at a time.

Social Situations or Presentations

If you feel nervous before a presentation or meeting new people, box breathing can help calm the "butterflies" and steady your mind. It's a quick, subtle way to regain control and enter the room with confidence.

DAY 11: VISUALIZATION FOR CALM

Visualization is a powerful technique that lets you create calmness from the inside out. When anxiety or stress kicks in, imagining a peaceful place can help you feel more grounded and relaxed, even if you're in the middle of a chaotic moment. Visualization works because your brain often responds to imagined scenarios as if they're real, so picturing a safe, calm space can actually help calm your body and mind It's like giving yourself a mental "vacation" where you feel safe and in control, no matter what's happening around you.

Choose Your Calm Place
Think of a place that feels peaceful to you. This could be somewhere you've actually been (like the beach, mountains, or your room) or an imaginary spot. Make it a place that brings you a sense of calm.

Close Your Eyes and Begin Visualizing
Get comfortable and close your eyes. Start imagining your calm place as if you're really there. Try to add as many details as you can to make it feel vivid and real.

Engage Your Senses
Imagine what you see, hear, feel, smell, and even taste in this place. Really immerse yourself in the scene

Take Slow, Deep Breaths

As you imagine this place, start taking slow, deep breaths. With each inhale, feel yourself relax more deeply into this scene. Imagine calmness spreading throughout your body.

Anchor the Calm Feeling

As you finish, remember how this calm place makes you feel. Open your eyes and try to bring a bit of that calmness with you as you return to the present.

Draw your calm place

Include the details that make it special to you. You can even keep this drawing handy as a reminder whenever you need a mental escape.

HOW TO USE VISUALIZATION FOR CALM IN EVERYDAY SITUATIONS

Facing Peer Pressure

When you feel pressured to do something you're uncomfortable with, pause for a moment and visualize your calm place. This can help you feel grounded, making it easier to say "no" and stick to what feels right for you.

Managing Shyness in New Situations

When walking into a new classroom, club, or social event, visualize your calm place beforehand to feel more at ease. Picture yourself confidently meeting people, which can help you feel more relaxed in new environments.

DAY 12: POSITIVE AFFIRMATIONS

Positive affirmations are statements that encourage self-belief and remind you of your strengths, especially on days when self-doubt creeps in. When anxiety, stress, or negative thoughts get in the way, affirmations act like a mental reset button, helping you stay focused on what's true and good about yourself.

Repeating affirmations regularly can help change the way you talk to yourself, building self-confidence and resilience over time. Think of affirmations as "mini pep talks" that help you keep a positive outlook, even during tough times.

WRITE AND REPEAT YOUR POSITIVE AFFIRMATIONS

Think about areas where you'd like more confidence or encouragement.
For example:

If you feel anxious about school, try: "I am capable and prepared to handle any challenge."

If you often doubt yourself, try: "I am enough, just as I am."

If you struggle with negative self-talk, try: "I am kind to myself, and I believe in my potential."

Write Down Your Affirmations

I am

I am

I am

Say Them Out Loud

Stand in front of a mirror if you can, and say each affirmation slowly and confidently. Imagine you're talking to a friend who needs encouragement. Repeat each one three times to really let it sink in.

Visualize Believing It

As you say each affirmation, try to feel it. Visualize what it would look like to embody that affirmation. Picture yourself succeeding, smiling, and feeling confident.

HOW TO USE AFFIRMATIONS DAILY

Starting Your Morning with Positivity
Repeating affirmations in the morning sets a positive tone for your day. Think of it as putting on "mental armor" that helps protect you from negative thoughts and self-doubt.

During Moments of Self-Doubt
When you catch yourself thinking, "I'm not good enough" or "I can't do this," replace it with an affirmation like "I am capable and resilient." This helps shift your mindset from self-criticism to self-support.

Ending the Day on a Positive Note
Reflect on your affirmations at night. Think about how they helped you throughout the day, and let that positivity carry you into a peaceful sleep.

DAY 13: PROGRESSIVE MUSCLE RELAXATION

Progressive Muscle Relaxation (PMR) is a technique that helps you release built-up tension and relax your entire body, one muscle group at a time. When you're feeling anxious or stressed, your body often reacts by tensing up—even if you don't notice it. PMR helps you notice where you're holding tension and teaches you how to let go of it.

PROGRESSIVE MUSCLE RELAXATION FROM HEAD TO TOE

Start with Your Face and Head
Tense: Squeeze the muscles in your face—your forehead, eyes, mouth, and jaw—then hold the tension for a count of 5.
Release: Let go of the tension, feeling your face soften and relax.

Move to Your Shoulders and Arms
Tense: Shrug your shoulders up toward your ears and clench your fists. Hold for a count of 5.
Release: Let your shoulders drop and your hands relax, noticing how much lighter they feel.

Chest and Stomach

Tense: Take a deep breath and tighten your chest and stomach muscles. Hold for 5 counts.
Release: Exhale slowly, letting the tension melt away as you relax these muscles.

Legs and Feet

Tense: Squeeze your thigh muscles and curl your toes. Hold the tension for a count of 5.
Release: Let your legs and feet relax, feeling grounded and calm.

End with a Full-Body Relaxation

Take one last deep breath, imagining any remaining tension leaving your body. Notice how your body feels—loose, relaxed, and at ease.

HOW TO USE PMR IN EVERYDAY SITUATIONS

While Feeling Anxious in Class

If anxiety hits during class—like before answering a question or giving a presentation—discreetly tense and relax your hands, arms, or shoulders. This can ease anxiety right there at your desk without drawing attention.

Easing Embarrassment or Shame

If something embarrassing happens, like making a mistake in class, use PMR to help reduce any physical tension or anxiety. This can make it easier to move on without dwelling on the incident. Discreetly tense and relax your hands or feet under the desk. Once you feel calmer, shift your attention back to the present.

DAY 14: LETTING GO OF WORRY THOUGHTS

When we're stressed or anxious, our minds tend to spiral with worry thoughts. These are often "what if" scenarios or fears about things we can't control. Letting go doesn't mean ignoring these thoughts; it means acknowledging them, sorting out what you can actually act on, and releasing the rest. This technique helps you focus on what's real and manageable instead of getting overwhelmed by the "what ifs."

By focusing only on what's within your control, you free yourself from unnecessary stress and create space for calm and confidence.

TAKE CONTROL OR LET GO

Step 1: Write Down Your Worries

Think about anything causing you stress, big or small—upcoming tests, friendships, or anything else.

Examples:
"What if I fail this test?"
"Will my friends still like me?"

Write it all down here.

Step 2: Sort Out What You Can and Can't Control

Look at each worry and ask, "Is this something I can control?" Mark each one as either "Take Action" or "Let Go".

Example: "Studying for the test" is something you can control (Take Action) , but "What if I fail?" isn't (Let Go).

Take Action	Let Go

Step 3: Focus on Your Action Plan

For the worries you labeled "Take Action", write one small step you can take to help ease your concern.

Example: "What if I fail this test?" Action: "Study one hour each day leading up to the test."

My Action Steps

☐ _____

☐ _____

☐ _____

Step 4: Practice Letting Go

For the worries you marked as "Let Go", imagine them drifting away. Visualize each worry as a balloon you release into the sky, or a wave washing it away.

HOW TO USE LETTING GO OF WORRIES IN EVERYDAY SITUATIONS

Dealing with Social Situations

Worried about what others think of you? Focus on what you can control—like being kind, listening, or participating. Let go of what you can't control, like other people's opinions or responses.

Facing a Big Game, Performance, or Presentation

If you're nervous before an event, make a plan to practice or review beforehand. Let go of thoughts like, "What if I mess up?" and focus on the actions that will help you feel prepared and confident.

DAY 15: SELF-REFLECTION ON ANXIETY MANAGEMENT

What Positive Changes Have You Noticed?	What Have You Learned About Your Triggers?
Describe any small victories or moments where you felt more in control.	Reflect on what types of situations or thoughts trigger your anxiety or strong emotions.

Which skill was the most helpful? Why?

SET YOUR INTENTION FOR NEXT WEEK
It could be practicing a particular skill daily or using an affirmation each morning.

PART 3: CONTROLLING IMPULSES WITH DISTRESS TOLERANCE SKILLS (DAYS 16-23)

Welcome to Part 3! This week, we're focusing on controlling impulses and handling those intense moments when emotions feel like they're taking over. Maybe it's the urge to lash out during an argument, stress-eat after a tough day, or say something you might regret later.

These reactions can feel hard to control, especially when anxiety or frustration is high.

Distress tolerance skills give you practical tools to help you manage these tough moments without reacting on impulse. These skills can help you stay calm, find balance, and handle stress in a healthier way. By practicing these, you'll be building up your ability to think before you act, making it easier to deal with whatever comes your way.

DAY 16: URGE SURFING

Today, we're exploring urge surfing—a skill that helps you manage strong urges without acting on them right away. Think about those moments when you feel a strong pull to check your phone during homework, snap at someone, or avoid a task. These urges can feel overwhelming, but urge surfing teaches you to handle them by letting them rise and fall, like waves. Imagine each urge as a wave that builds up and then calms down. Your goal is to "ride" the wave until it passes, showing yourself that you're in control. Ready to give it a try? Let's ride those waves!

URGE SURFING: RIDE THE WAVE

Step 1: Notice the Urge

Think of a recent urge you had—like checking your phone, avoiding homework, or saying something impulsive. Write it down here.

Example: "I feel the urge to check my phone."

_____

_____

_____

_____

Step 2: Describe the Urge

What does this urge feel like? Is it a strong pull? Restless energy? Jittery hands? Write down any physical sensations.

Example: "It feels like a tightness in my chest and an itch to grab my phone."

_____

_____

_____

_____

Step 3: Breathe Through It

Take a few deep breaths. Imagine each breath helping you stay balanced on top of the "urge wave." With each breath, draw a wave line below to represent yourself riding it.

Wave Line: Draw each wave as you breathe

Step 4: Stay with the Urge

Imagine yourself "surfing" on this urge. Tell yourself, **"This urge will pass."** Write that phrase here to remind yourself:

Keep breathing and notice as the urge starts to fade. Describe how it feels as it slowly loses power.
Example: "The tightness in my chest is softening, and the urge isn't as strong."
Your Observation:

_____
_____
_____
_____

Step 5: Celebrate Your Success
When the urge passes without you acting on it, give yourself a mental high-five! Write one thing you feel proud of about staying in control.

_____
_____
_____
_____

When to Use Urge Surfing

Resisting the Urge to Procrastinate

You know you need to start a big assignment, but the urge to avoid it is strong. Instead of acting on that urge, acknowledge it: "I feel the urge to procrastinate." Visualize yourself surfing over it, letting it rise and fall as you breathe.

Handling an Urge to Snap at Someone

If a friend or family member says something that irritates you, you might feel the impulse to react sharply. Pause, take a breath, and notice the urge to respond immediately. Let the feeling pass like a wave, and choose a calm response instead.

Day 17: Pause and Choose

Today's skill is Pause and Choose—a tool that helps you slow down and think before you react. When emotions run high, especially in stressful or tense situations, it's easy to say or do something impulsively that you might regret later. Pause and Choose gives you the power to step back, consider the outcomes, and decide on a response that feels right.

Think of it as hitting the "pause" button on a remote. Just like you'd pause a show to get a snack or rewind, pausing in real life helps you reset before you decide what to do next. It's a simple but powerful way to stay in control, especially when anxiety or emotions feel overwhelming. Ready to give it a try? Let's go!

Practicing Pause and Choose

Step 1: Pause
Stop what you're doing, take a deep breath, and give yourself a moment to slow down.

Step 2: Check Your Feelings
Describe your feelings in this moment
Examples: Frustrated, annoyed, nervous
Where do you feel it in your body?
Examples: tight chest, clenched fists

_____
_____
_____

Step 3: Consider the Outcomes

Imagine two different paths: write what might happen if you pause and respond or act on your first impulse in each pathway.

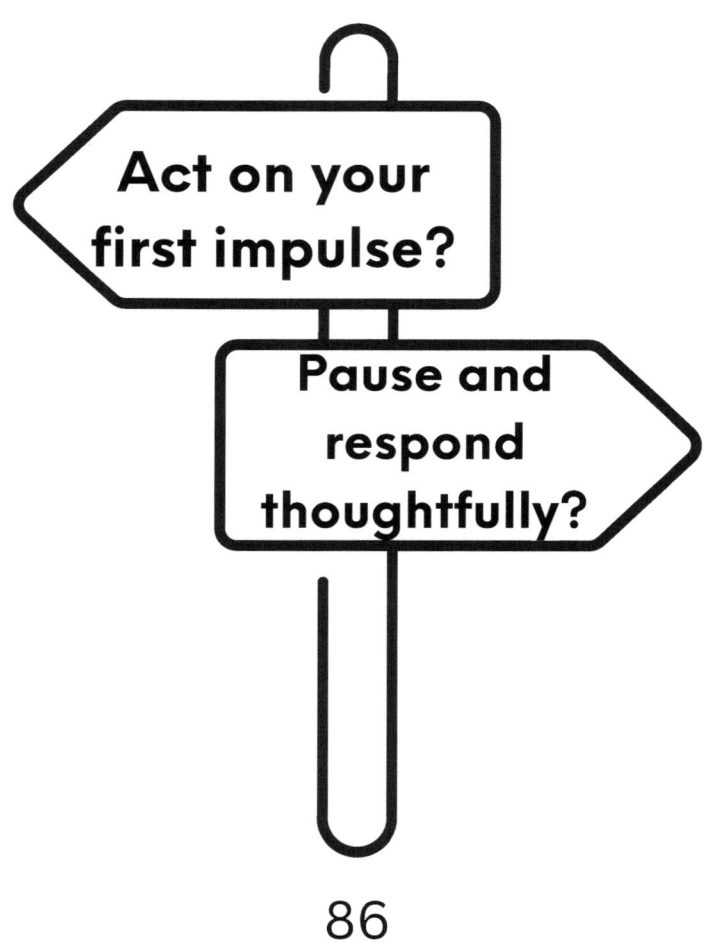

Step 4: Choose Your Action

Now, pick the option that feels better for you. Choose something you'll be proud of later, not just what feels satisfying in the moment. Select the choice that feels right for you and explain why it's a good choice. What action will you choose?

- [ ] Take a deep breath and calmly explain how I feel.
- [ ] Walk away to give myself a break and calm down.
- [ ] Ask for help or advice from someone I trust.
- [ ] Focus on something else to distract myself.
- [ ] Hold off on responding and revisit the situation when I feel calmer.

How and When to Use Pause and Choose

When Receiving Criticism or Feedback

If someone criticizes you (like a teacher, coach, or friend), the urge might be to defend yourself or feel hurt. Pause for a second to consider the feedback and ask yourself if there's anything constructive to learn from it. Respond thoughtfully instead of jumping to conclusions.

Before Making a Big Decision

If you're feeling unsure about a choice—like committing to a new activity, saying "yes" to something you're unsure about, or even buying something you want—Pause and check in with yourself. Take a moment to consider the pros and cons before moving forward.

Day 18: Breaking Down Tasks

Ever looked at a huge assignment or project and felt totally overwhelmed? You're not alone. Big tasks can feel impossible, especially when anxiety or stress kicks in. Today, we're focusing on **Breaking Down Tasks**—a skill that helps you tackle anything, no matter how big, by breaking it into smaller, manageable steps.

Think of it like putting together a puzzle. Instead of trying to handle everything at once, you'll take it one piece at a time.

This makes things feel way more doable and way less overwhelming.

Breaking Down a Big Task into Small Steps

Write down something that's been stressing you out. This could be anything, like studying for a test, finishing a project, or cleaning your room.

Your Task:

_____

_____

Step 1: Break It Down
List the mini steps that make up your task, like pieces of a puzzle.

Example:
Research
Create an outline
Write introduction

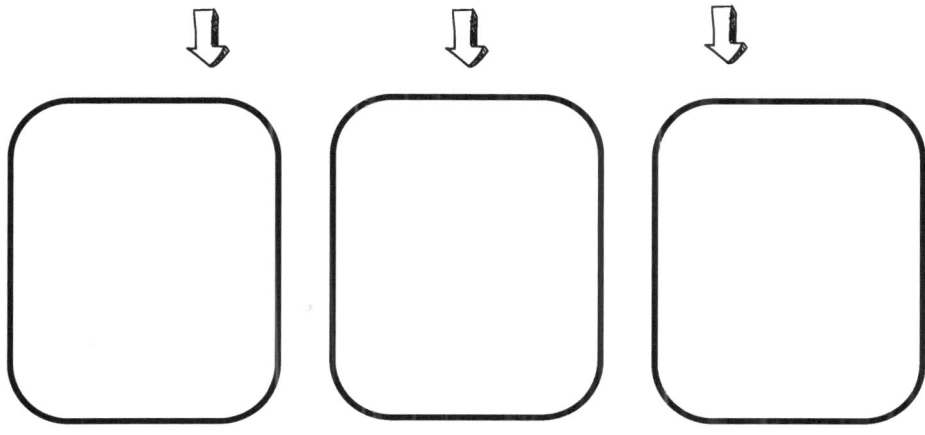

Step 2: Time It!
Give each mini step a realistic time limit. Set a timer on your phone to help you stay on track.

Example: "I'll spend 20 minutes on each research article."

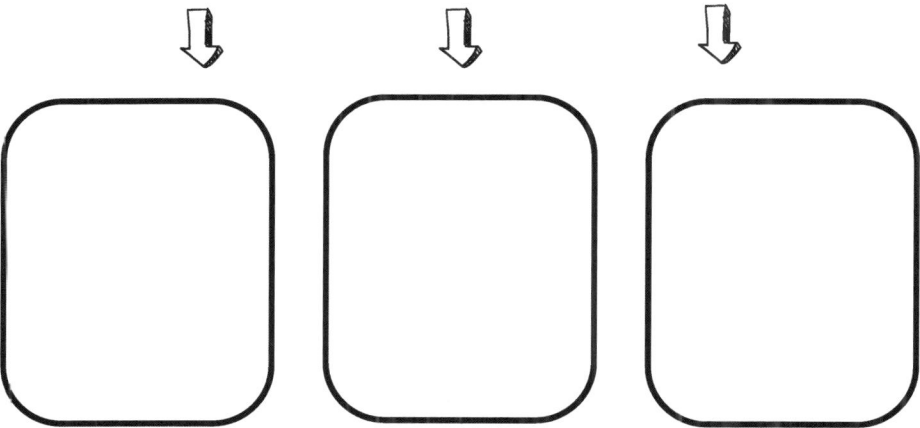

Step 3: Start Small

Pick your first step and focus only on that. Cross it off when you're done, then move to the next.

Step 4: Reward Yourself

After each mini step, reward yourself with something fun to stay motivated.
Example Rewards:
Watch a funny TikTok or reel
Grab a handful of your favorite snack
Listen to your favorite song
Text a friend for a quick chat
Take a short walk around the room

My Reward:

_____

_____

Using breaking down tasks Every Day

Coping with Emotional Overwhelm or Anxiety Spikes

If you feel an emotional wave coming on (like anxiety, sadness, or anger), breaking down your coping methods can help you manage the moment.

Steps:
Take deep breaths to calm your body.
Write down how you're feeling or vent in a journal.
Identify a small action that will help (like taking a walk or talking to a friend).
Reward yourself with something soothing, like listening to your favorite song, after you've calmed down.

Breaking down your response to emotional overwhelm helps you manage anxiety, keeps impulse reactions in check, and supports emotional health.

Dealing with Exam Stress Over a Longer Period

If you have a big exam coming up in a few weeks, use task management to create a study plan.

Steps:

Break down each subject into smaller topics or units.
Assign certain topics to different days of the week.
Schedule review sessions for past topics to reinforce memory.
Take practice quizzes or do flashcards as small study rewards.

By spacing out your study sessions, you reduce the urge to cram last minute, lowering anxiety and building confidence.

Day 19: Managing Distractions

We all get distracted, especially with things like homework or chores. Between notifications and social media, staying focused can feel impossible! But when distractions pull us away from what we need to do, it often leads to last-minute stress, missed deadlines, and feeling overwhelmed. Today's skill, Focus and Distraction Management, helps you identify your biggest distractions and find ways to manage them. Practicing this will keep you on track, reduce anxiety, and give you more control over your time. Ready to take control? Let's dive in!

Identify Your Distractions and Develop a Strategy

Step 1: Identify Your Top 3 Distractions
Think about what usually pulls you away from tasks like studying or homework.

Step 2: Create Your Distraction Strategies
For each distraction, come up with 1-2 strategies to help you stay focused.

Example:
   Phone: Turn on "Do Not Disturb" mode or set a timer to check your phone only every 30 minutes.
   Other People: Let family know you're working or use headphones.
   Thoughts: Write down distracting thoughts to come back to later, or take a few deep breaths to refocus.

Distraction	Strategy

Step 3: Try Out Your Plan

Pick a task to work on today, and test out your distraction strategies.

Use Focus and Distraction Management Daily

When Feeling Overwhelmed or Anxious

If anxious thoughts keep popping up, use your notebook to jot them down and "save" them for later. Remind yourself that you can revisit these thoughts after you're done with your task.

In Social Situations

If you're easily distracted by what's happening around you, practice mindful listening. Give your full attention to the person speaking by putting your phone away, making eye contact, and focusing on their words. This can help improve your relationships and reduce social anxiety.

Studying for Exams

If studying is hard because your phone keeps pulling your attention, use the "Do Not Disturb" mode or keep your phone in a different room for 30-minute study blocks. This can help you focus better, avoid last-minute stress, and feel prepared.

Day 20: Mindful Eating

When we're stressed, anxious, or feeling down, it's easy to rush through meals without really tasting the food or noticing when we're full. Sometimes we even eat out of boredom or to distract ourselves from tough emotions. Mindful Eating is a skill that helps you slow down and enjoy your food, while also learning to listen to your body and control impulses.

Today's practice is about eating in a way that helps you stay present, appreciate each bite, and build self-control. By practicing mindful eating, you can feel more connected to your body and even reduce stress and anxiety. Ready to give it a try? Let's dig in!

Practicing Mindful Eating

Choose a small snack, sit somewhere calm, and put away distractions (yes, even your phone!).
My Snack:
_____

Notice Your Food with All Senses
Look: What colors and textures stand out?
Smell: Take a slow sniff—what does it remind you of?
Touch: Feel its texture. Is it soft, crunchy, smooth?
Listen: Does it make a sound when you pick it up or bite?

Take a Slow, Intentional Bite

Place a bite in your mouth and let it sit there for a moment. Notice the flavor, texture, and temperature. Try to make each bite last at least 10 seconds. This slow approach helps you stay in control, rather than rushing through your food impulsively.

Body Check-In

After your first bite, pause to ask yourself: "Am I actually hungry, or am I eating for another reason?" Rate your fullness level from 1 to 5.

Continue Slowly

Keep eating one bite at a time, putting your food down between each bite. Check in with yourself periodically to see how you're feeling.

Using Mindful Eating to Manage Emotions and Impulses

Dealing with Emotional Highs and Lows
When emotions run high, it's tempting to use food for comfort. Mindful eating helps you pause and check in with yourself before, during, and after eating, so you're more aware of your emotions and can choose healthier ways to cope, like deep breathing or talking to a friend.

Handling Impulsive Cravings
If you get the urge to snack when you're not hungry, mindful eating lets you pause and ask, "Am I really hungry, or is this just a habit?" This builds impulse control and can help with managing other habits, like checking your phone in class.

When You're Feeling Anxious
Anxiety often leads us to look for quick comforts. Mindful eating helps you slow down, focus on each bite, and avoid mindless eating to calm your nerves, making you feel more in control and less rushed.

Day 21: Technology Boundaries

Let's be real: technology is awesome, but it can also be a huge distraction. When we're glued to our screens, it's easy for anxiety, stress, or even FOMO (fear of missing out) to creep in. Setting boundaries with technology can help you feel more balanced, reduce stress, and stay focused on things that matter.

Today's skill will help you take control of your screen time, so you can enjoy what you love online without it taking over your day. Ready to set some boundaries and feel more in control? Let's do this!

Set a Screen Time Limit for One Day

Step 1: Choose Your Limit

Decide on a screen time limit that's realistic but challenging.

Example Limits:

Only check your phone on the hour
30 minutes of YouTube during study breaks

My Limit:

Step 2: Set Boundaries

Use your phone's screen time settings, an app, or set an alarm to help stick to your limit.

Step 3: Plan Offline Activities

Write down a few things you'll do instead of reaching for your phone.

Activities List

1. _____
2. _____
3. _____

Step 4: End-of-Day Reflection

Afterward, take a few minutes to reflect:

How did limiting screen time impact your mood?

Did you feel more focused or less anxious?

_____
_____
_____
_____
_____
_____
_____
_____

Scenarios for Technology Boundaries

Handling FOMO (Fear of Missing Out)
Constantly checking notifications can increase FOMO and stress. By setting boundaries, you're teaching yourself that it's okay to miss a few updates. Instead, focus on things happening around you in real life.

Managing Impulses to Check Your Phone in Social Settings
If you find it hard to resist your phone around friends, try setting a rule for yourself, like "No phones at dinner" or "Phone-free hangouts." This can help you stay present and build stronger connections.

Managing Social Media Stress
If you feel anxious after scrolling through social media, set a daily limit to help. Use that extra time to focus on something that makes you feel good, like hanging out with friends or spending time on a hobby.

Day 22: Counting Technique

Sometimes emotions hit us hard and fast—like when you're frustrated with a friend, stressed about school, or just feeling overwhelmed. In those moments, it's easy to react without thinking, often saying or doing something we might regret later.

The counting technique is a simple but powerful tool to help you pause, breathe, and give yourself a moment to choose how to respond. By counting to 10, you're giving yourself a mini "cool-off" period, so you stay in control instead of letting your impulses take over.

This skill can make a big difference in helping you handle tough emotions with more calm and confidence.

Count to 10 Before Reacting

Recognize the Impulse
Notice the urge to react—whether it's anger, checking your phone, or reacting to someone's comment.

Count to 10 Slowly
Close your eyes if possible and count to 10, creating a "pause" between the urge and your response.

Take a Deep Breath
After counting, take one deep breath to help ground yourself.

Choose Your Response
Think, "Will this choice help or make things worse?" Pick the response that feels better for you.

Using the Counting Technique

After a Mistake or Embarrassing Moment
If you mess up or feel embarrassed, the immediate impulse might be to hide or react out of frustration. Try counting to 10 and remind yourself that everyone makes mistakes. Then, choose a response that helps you move forward instead of dwelling on it.

In an Argument with Friends or Family
Let's say you're in a disagreement with a friend or family member, and you feel yourself getting angry. Instead of saying something hurtful, use the counting technique to pause, calm down, and respond in a way that won't hurt the relationship.

By practicing the counting technique, you're training yourself to pause, think, and make choices that work in your favour, even when emotions run high. Give it a try and see how it helps you stay in control!

Day 23: Reflecting on Impulse Control

Identify Challenges and Triggers	Celebrate Small Wins
Think of situations where it was hard to stay in control.	Write down a few examples where you felt proud of your self-control.

Which skill was the most helpful? Why?

SET YOUR INTENTION FOR NEXT WEEK

Examples: "When I feel the urge to check my phone during homework, I'll count to 10 and then decide."

Part 4: Boosting Emotional Health with Interpersonal Effectiveness Skills (Days 24-30)

Hey there! You've made it to the last part of this journey—amazing work! This week, it's all about building stronger, healthier connections with the people around you. We'll dive into skills that help you speak up for yourself, set boundaries, and handle conflicts without stress.

If you've been feeling anxious, struggling with impulse control, or just dealing with a lot of emotions, these skills can make things feel a lot easier in social situations. Over the next seven days, you'll learn ways to improve communication, feel more confident in your relationships, and stay true to yourself. Let's level up those connection skills and take on this final week together!

Day 24: Practicing Gratitude

Gratitude may sound simple, but it's one of the most powerful ways to lift your mood and improve emotional health. When you're dealing with anxiety, intense emotions, or impulsive reactions, it's easy to focus on what's going wrong.

Practicing gratitude is about shifting that focus to what's going right, even if it's just the little things. This could be anything—a good conversation, something that made you laugh, or even a small victory in your day. Focusing on these moments can help you feel calmer, more positive, and more in control.

Ready to boost your mood? Let's get started!

Daily Gratitude Journal

List Three Things You're Grateful For
Every day, take a moment to write down three things you're grateful for. This could be anything—from big wins like doing well on a test, to small things like a funny meme or a delicious snack. Even on tough days, there are usually tiny moments to appreciate!

Example:
My friend made me laugh during lunch.
I got through my math homework without feeling too stressed.
My favorite song came on when I needed a mood boost.

My Gratitude List for Today:

1._____
2._____
3._____

Using Gratitude to Handle Stressful Moments

At the End of a Rough Day
On days that feel overwhelming, gratitude can help you shift perspective. List three small positives before bed, like a nice meal, a funny moment, or even just getting through a hard day. This small practice can make you feel more balanced and ready for tomorrow.

When You're Feeling Down
If you're in a low mood, gratitude can give you a quick mental boost. Looking for positives—even tiny ones—can help you feel a bit better, even if it doesn't fix everything.

When you're nervous about something new
Joining a club, trying out for a team, or presenting—pause and list a few things you're grateful for, like supportive friends, past successes, or strengths in yourself. This helps calm nerves and boosts confidence.

Day 25: Visualization for Success

Have you ever pictured something awesome happening before it actually does—like nailing a presentation, winning a game, or just feeling confident walking into a room? That's called visualization, and it's a powerful tool to build confidence and reduce anxiety. When you're dealing with big emotions, impulses, or self-doubt, visualizing success can help you feel ready to take on challenges.

Today's skill is all about "seeing" yourself succeed before you even begin. You'll use this to imagine yourself achieving a goal, like doing well on a test, handling a stressful situation calmly, or giving an amazing presentation. The more vividly you can picture it, the more your mind will believe it's possible—and that belief can help you perform better when the time comes. Ready to give it a try? Let's dive in!

Picture Your Success

1. Choose a Goal
Think of an upcoming challenge—like acing a test or staying calm in a stressful situation.

5. Feel the Achievement
Imagine the pride or relief as you accomplish your goal. Hold onto that positive feeling.

2. Get Comfortable
Sit in a quiet spot, close your eyes, and take a few deep breaths to relax.

3. Visualize the Scene
Imagine the details vividly. Picture yourself in the room, focused and calm

4. Imagine Success
See yourself handling everything smoothly, calm and in control. Let any nerves fade into focus and confidence.

When to Use Visualization

Managing Test Anxiety
Picture yourself reading questions calmly, solving problems one by one, and feeling steady as you work through each part of the test.

Getting Through Challenging Conversations
If you need to have a tough talk with a friend or family member, visualize yourself staying calm, listening, and expressing yourself clearly and confidently.

Handling Impulse Control
If you're struggling with the urge to check your phone while studying, visualize yourself staying focused, finishing your task, and feeling accomplished afterward.

Dealing with Social Situations
If you feel nervous in group settings, picture yourself staying calm, listening confidently, and enjoying the moment. Imagine feeling comfortable just as you are.

Day 26: Acts of Kindness

Ever notice how doing something nice for someone else can make you feel surprisingly good? Practicing small acts of kindness isn't just about helping others—it actually helps you, too! When you're feeling anxious, overwhelmed, or just down, showing kindness can shift your focus, lift your mood, and even strengthen your relationships.

Today's skill is all about putting a little extra positivity out there. By focusing on kindness, you're not only boosting your own emotional health, but you're also building stronger connections with the people around you. Think of it as a double win: making someone's day a little better, while also helping yourself feel calmer and happier.

Do One Small Kind Act for Someone

Think of something simple you can do for someone today.
Here are some ideas:

Compliment a Friend: Tell a friend something you genuinely like about them.
Help Out at Home: Offer to help with a chore or make someone a snack.
Write a Note of Encouragement: Leave a sticky note for someone in your family or a friend.
Be a Good Listener: Take a few minutes to really listen to someone who needs to talk.
Share a Positive Text or Meme: Send something uplifting to a friend who might be having a tough day.

Once you've picked an act, go ahead and do it! Pay attention to how it feels—does being kind make you feel lighter, more positive, or connected? Notice if it helps shift any negative feelings.

When to Use Kindness in Everyday Life

When You're Feeling Anxious
Acts of kindness can distract you from your own worries by focusing on helping others. It can also make you feel more connected and supported.

If You're Frustrated or Impulsive
Practicing kindness helps you pause and think of others, giving you space to make thoughtful choices instead of reacting impulsively.

When You're Feeling Down or Lonely
Kindness can lift your mood and strengthen connections with friends or family, making you feel less isolated.

Day 27: Journaling for Emotional Release

Ever feel like your mind's racing with too many thoughts or emotions? Sometimes, just getting everything out on paper can be a huge relief. Journaling is like having a personal space where you can say anything you want without judgment. When things feel overwhelming, or when you're dealing with anxiety, frustration, or impulse control, journaling can help you sort through it all.

Today's skill focuses on using journaling to let your thoughts and feelings flow freely. It's about letting go of whatever's bottled up inside—whether that's worries about school, tension with friends, or just something that's been on your mind. Think of it as clearing space in your mind so you feel lighter and more in control.

Write Freely About Your Feelings

Use a notebook or a notes app on your phone, whatever feels easiest. Write whatever comes to mind, even if it seems messy or unorganized. Some days, you might want to talk about what happened that day, how someone made you feel, or what's stressing you out. Here are some prompts to get started:

Today, I feel...
I'm worried about...
One thing that's been bothering me is...
If I could change one thing about today, it would be...

Once you've written, take a moment to look over what you wrote and notice if any themes or patterns stand out. Sometimes, just seeing your thoughts on paper can help you realize what you need, or it might help you decide on one small action you could take to feel better.

When to Use Journaling

When You're Angry or Frustrated
Instead of reacting impulsively, write about why you're upset. This pause to reflect can help you feel calmer and more in control of your reaction.

To Track Emotional Patterns
If you journal regularly, look back at what you've written to spot patterns. Are there certain things that stress you out over and over? Recognizing these can help you make changes.

After a Tough Day at School
Maybe you had a difficult class or felt left out with friends. Use journaling as a way to let out your frustrations without holding anything back.

Day 28: Catching Wins

We all go through days where it feels like everything's going wrong, or maybe nothing's going as planned. But even on the tough days, there are small victories—things you accomplished or moments you handled well. Catching Wins is about noticing those little successes that can boost your mood, keep you motivated, and remind you that you're making progress, even if it doesn't always feel that way.

Whether you managed to focus on studying for ten extra minutes, talked yourself through a moment of anxiety, or held back on a quick impulse, those are all wins worth celebrating! Noticing these small accomplishments can help you build confidence, feel good about yourself, and stay on track.

My Wins

Every evening, take a few minutes to think back on the day and write down three small wins. They don't have to be huge! Even little moments count as wins if they helped you feel good or improved your day.

Example Wins:
"I kept my focus during a study session without checking my phone."

"I took a few deep breaths instead of reacting right away when I felt frustrated."

"I talked to a friend about something on my mind, and it helped me feel less stressed."

Everyday Moments Where Catching Wins Can Be Helpful

Recognizing Positive Self-Talk Moments
Negative thoughts about yourself can feel overwhelming, especially when you're anxious.
If you catch yourself replacing a negative thought with a more positive one, write that down. Seeing these moments as wins reinforces self-compassion.

Getting Through Tough Conversations
You have an emotionally charged conversation with a friend or family member and feel nervous about staying calm.
If you managed to stay respectful and focused on expressing yourself without reacting impulsively, that's a win to celebrate!

Day 29: Future Self Visualization

Today, let's take a trip to your future! Visualizing your future self is about imagining what you can achieve when you put in the effort and stay focused on your goals. It's like having a preview of all the things you're working towards—whether it's becoming more confident, staying calm in tough moments, or just feeling proud of how far you've come.

For those of us who sometimes feel anxious, impulsive, or overwhelmed, picturing our future selves achieving something big can be super motivating. It's like sending a message to yourself that you can get through the challenges and that every small step you take today brings you closer to where you want to be.

✦ Imagine Your Future Self

Think about something you want to achieve, like staying calm during a test, feeling confident in a social situation, or handling stress better.

My Goal

What's one small action you can do today to get closer to this future self?

Imagine how great it will feel to succeed. What emotions will you experience?

Close your eyes and imagine the details. Where are you? What are you doing? How do you feel?

Everyday Ways to Use Future Self Visualization

Dealing with Drama

Friendship drama happens. If you're nervous about a conversation, picture yourself staying calm, expressing your feelings clearly, and handling it maturely. Imagine feeling proud for staying in control and saying what matters most.

Handling Emotional Ups and Downs

Picture your future self managing emotions calmly, like taking deep breaths instead of snapping at a friend or shutting down. This reinforces that you're capable of making thoughtful choices.

Dealing with a Tough Day

If you're overwhelmed after a long day, visualize your future self relaxing at the end of it, knowing you handled everything with strength and calm. This shifts your focus from stress to the relief of overcoming it.

Day 30: Celebrating and Reflecting on Progress

Congrats—you made it! Today's all about taking a moment to look back at everything you've learned, how far you've come, and how much stronger you've become. Sometimes when you're dealing with anxiety, impulse control, or emotional ups and downs, it's easy to focus on what's still hard. But it's just as important to notice and celebrate your wins—even the small ones.

Reflecting helps you see what's working, what you're proud of, and how you can keep building on those successes. So, let's dive into this final step together, because you've earned it!

Write down 3 things you're proud of	Highlight Your Favorite Skill
	Think about which skill made the biggest difference in your life.

What was one tough moment where you used a skill to handle it?

SET A FUTURE GOAL
Now that you've built these skills, what's one area of your life where you want to keep improving?

Your Journey Doesn't End Here

You did it! 30 days of learning, growing, and taking steps to understand yourself better. Whether you were tackling anxiety, managing impulses, or boosting your emotional health, you've made incredible progress.

Life isn't always easy, and challenges will keep coming, but now you've got tools to handle them. From mindfulness and self-reflection to grounding techniques and gratitude, you've built a toolkit to help you stay calm, confident, and in control, no matter what life throws your way.

This book may end here, but your journey doesn't. Keep practicing these skills—whether it's pausing before reacting, focusing on small wins, or visualizing your future self—and watch how they help you handle tough moments. Remember, it's not about being perfect. It's about showing up for yourself, trying your best, and learning as you go.

You don't have to do this alone. Share what you've learned with people you trust—friends, family, or even a counselor—and let them support you. You've taken the first steps toward becoming the best version of yourself, and that's something to celebrate.

Life is a journey, not a race. Take it one step at a time, and don't forget to be kind to yourself along the way. You're stronger, wiser, and more capable than you might realize. Keep showing up for yourself. You've got this!

Extra Writing Space

Extra Writing Space

Extra Writing Space

Extra Writing Space

Extra Writing Space